COMPREHENSION

MAIN IDEA

LEVEL B

Linda Ward Beech

Tara McCarthy

Donna Townsend

STECK-VAUGHN
ELEMENTARY · SECONDARY · ADULT · LIBRARY

A Harcourt Company

www.steck-vaughn.com

Editorial Director:	Diane Schnell
Project Editor:	Anne Souby
Associate Director of Design:	Cynthia Ellis
Design Manager:	Cynthia Hannon
Media Researcher:	Christina Berry
Production:	Karen Wilburn
Cover Illustration:	Stephanie Carter
Cover Production:	Alan Klemp
Photograph:	©Wonderfile

ISBN 0-7398-2631-X

2 3 4 5 6 7 8 9 0 BNG 04 03 02 01

The main idea is the point a writer tries to make. In this book you will learn about main ideas.

Look at the picture. What do you think of when you say "farm"? Do you think of a barn like the one in the picture? There are sunflowers growing by this barn. There are also fields around the barn. The farm is the main idea of this picture. The barn and the sunflowers are details. They make this picture look like a farm.

What Is a Main Idea?

The main idea of a story tells what the whole story is about. Each story in this book has a main idea. It is usually one sentence somewhere in each story.

Why do stories have sentences other than the main idea sentence? The other sentences are *details*. They tell you more about the main idea. They also make the story more fun to read.

The example below may help you think about main ideas. All the details add up to the main idea.

detail + detail + detail = main idea

3 + 4 + 5 = 12

The *3*, *4*, and *5* are like details. They add up to the main idea. The main idea is like the *12*. It is bigger than the details. It is made up of many smaller parts.

Try It!

Read the story below. Draw a line under the main idea.

Do you sing in the bathtub? Do you sing in the car? Here's how you can become a singing star! You can go to a store. Someone will play music while you sing a song. Then the people there will make a recording of your song. You can take it home and surprise your friends!

Steck-Vaughn • Comprehension Skills Series

How to Choose a Main Idea

The main idea of the story is the sentence about becoming a singing star. All the other sentences are details. They tell how you can become a star. Write the details on the lines below.

Detail 1: You might sing in the _____

or in the _____ .

Detail 2: You can go to a _____ .

Detail 3: Someone will play _____ .

Detail 4: The people will make a _____
of your song.

Detail 5: You can _____
your friends.

Now write the main idea on the lines below. It is the sentence that is not a detail.

Main Idea: _____

_____

◆ What do all the sentences add up to? Remember that the main idea is bigger than the details. It is made up of many smaller parts.
◆ Read each story. As you read, think about each sentence. Does it tell only a small part of the whole story? If it does, it is a detail. Does it tell what the story is about? Then it is the main idea.

To check your answers, turn to page 60.

Practice Finding the Main Idea

This book is filled with stories. Each story has a main idea. You will be asked to find these main ideas.

Read the stories below. Then answer the questions.

◆

> The male flag bird does not have to look for a mate. He is so pretty that a mate will come looking for him. He has long feathers around his neck. His flags are on his head. *Flags* are bright feathers. They shine and wave as he dances in the trees.

___*A*___ **1.** The story mainly tells
- **A.** how pretty the male flag bird is
- **B.** what flags are like
- **C.** how the flag bird dances

The correct answer is **A**. One sentence says that "He is so pretty that a mate will come looking for him." The other sentences add details about his pretty feathers.

◆

> The Bill of Rights says that people are free to talk about anything. People can talk about things they like and don't like. The Bill of Rights is important in our lives. It helps us stay free.

_____ **2.** The story mainly tells
- **A.** what kinds of things people say
- **B.** how people change bad things
- **C.** what the Bill of Rights is about

To check your answer, turn to page 60.

How to Use This Book

Read the stories in this book. Each story has a main idea. Think about each question. Then choose the correct answer.

You can check your answers by yourself. If you wish, tear out pages 61 and 62. Find the unit you want to check. Fold the answer page on the dotted line to show the correct unit. Count the number of correct answers. Write that number in the score box at the top of the page.

Hints for Better Reading

◆ As you read ask yourself, "Is this sentence a main idea? Or is this sentence a detail?"

◆ Think about which sentence is bigger than all of the details.

Challenge Yourself

Read each story. Then write a title for each story. Make sure that the title tells what the story is about.

Writing

On pages 30 and 58, there are stories with questions. These do not have answers for you to choose. Think of an answer. Write it in your own words. On pages 31 and 59, you are asked to write your own story. You are given a prewriting activity to help you. You will find suggested answers on page 60. But your answers may be very different.

1. Baseball teams buy new balls for big games. But the new balls are slippery. So before each game, someone puts mud on them. But it's a special kind of mud. It makes the balls easier to use.

2. Baby frogs grow from eggs. The mother frog lays her eggs in a pond. The dark center of each egg grows a tail. The eggs have no shells, so the young frog soon starts wiggling around. The baby frog looks like a fish. It swims with its tail and eats tiny water plants. Later it grows four legs and loses its tail. It learns to live both on land and in water.

3. For a long time, sailors have known that sea plants help heal cuts or sores. Now someone has made sea plants into a kind of bandage. It keeps dirt out of skin cuts. It also helps cuts heal.

4. Look at the back of a dollar bill. You will find a circle with an eagle in it. That is the Great Seal of the United States. What do the parts of the seal stand for? The eagle is a strong bird. It stands for might. The bird holds a branch and some arrows. The branch stands for peace. The arrows stand for war. The eagle has a ribbon in its mouth. The writing on the ribbon says, "Out of many states, one nation."

_____ **1.** The story mainly tells
        A. why ball players put mud on new balls
        B. where the baseball mud comes from
        C. when mud takes care of problems

_____ **2.** The story mainly tells
        A. how frogs grow from eggs
        B. why eggs have dark centers
        C. what eats tiny water plants

_____ **3.** The story mainly tells
        A. how sea water keeps dirt out of cuts
        B. why sailors are always hurting themselves
        C. how sea plants are used to heal cuts

_____ **4.** The story mainly tells
        A. what is on the front of a dollar bill
        B. what the parts of the Great Seal stand for
        C. what the ribbon on the dollar says

1. It's easy to go up in a hot-air balloon. It's harder to come down. A gas burner heats the air inside a hot-air balloon. The hot air rises. So does the balloon. But what if people in the balloon want to come down? They have to wait for the air in the balloon to cool. Then the balloon slowly falls. They throw out ropes. Then the balloon is pulled to the ground.

2. People can almost fly like birds. To do this, they fly planes called gliders. Gliders have no engines. All the pilot hears is the rush of the wind. Warm air keeps the gliders up. As the air rises, it takes the glider with it. To find warm air, pilots watch for birds. Birds like to glide in warm air, too.

3. Dogs make good pets. But picking the right dog is no easy task. There are more than 400 breeds of dogs. Small ones can weigh fewer than 3 pounds. Big ones can weigh more than 150 pounds. Sometimes dogs help with the picking. They bark at the owner they want.

4. Older Americans have more power today than before. For a long time, older people couldn't work. Everyone thought that they were too old. Older people couldn't get the help they needed. But then they got together. They worked for the things they wanted. They helped each other. And they voted for people who would listen to them.

_____ **1.** The story mainly tells

      A. how hot-air balloons go up and down

      B. who rides hot-air balloons

      C. when a hot-air balloon needs air

_____ **2.** The story mainly tells

      A. how birds glide in the wind

      B. how warm air can be

      C. how people can fly like birds

_____ **3.** The story mainly tells

      A. who picked a pet

      B. about picking a pet dog

      C. how dogs bark

_____ **4.** The story mainly tells

      A. who was too old to get a job

      B. why older Americans have more power

      C. who got together to form clubs

1. We make sounds by changing the shape of our mouth and throat. Do birds sing this way? Most people did not think so. But scientists have learned that birds sing different notes by changing the shape of their throats. It seems as if they sing like people.

2. Bus companies were getting worried. Fewer and fewer passengers were riding the buses. Then someone had an idea. Airplanes show movies on long trips. Buses on long trips could show movies, too. Some buses now show movies. More people are riding these buses. Today these bus companies have more riders.

3. Turtles have been on Earth for millions of years. Most turtles have hard shells. But a few types of turtles have soft shells. Some turtles spend almost all their time in the water. Others spend most of their time on land. So turtles are not all alike. But they are all hatched from eggs. And all turtle eggs are laid on land.

4. Hattie Wyatt Caraway did something new in 1932. She became the first woman elected to the United States Senate. And she did a good job. The people liked her. The next time she ran, Senator Caraway won again.

_____ **1.** The story mainly tells
- **A.** how people and birds sing
- **B.** who uses air to make words
- **C.** why people like to sing

_____ **2.** The story mainly tells
- **A.** who takes buses on long trips
- **B.** how bus companies got more riders
- **C.** when airplanes show the most movies

_____ **3.** The story mainly tells
- **A.** about different turtles
- **B.** which turtles live long
- **C.** how much a turtle egg weighs

_____ **4.** The story mainly tells
- **A.** how senators are elected
- **B.** about the first woman senator
- **C.** about life in 1932

1. Young squirrels like to eat the bark of trees. They pull the bark off trees and eat the sweet juices. Eating too much bark can kill a squirrel. Why do they do it? To them, it's squirrel candy.

2. Sometimes people hurt things when they don't mean to. The southern part of Florida used to be mostly water. Then people came to live there. They built dams and canals. Much of the water drained away. Farmers could farm the land. Hunters could hunt the animals there. But many of the animals that once lived in this place have left. They needed lots of water to live.

3. Scientists used to think that all raindrops were small. They thought that big drops of water would bump into each other as they fell from the clouds. By the time they reached the ground, they would be small raindrops. But other scientists took pictures of raindrops. Many raindrops were as big as your finger.

4. Most plants need a rest every year. How can you tell when a plant is resting? Most plants outdoors rest in winter. Some outdoor plants drop their leaves during this time. Other plants stop growing. Indoor plants rest, too. They grow more slowly while they rest. They do not need much food and water. They also may not grow any flowers until it is time to stop resting.

_____ **1.** The story mainly tells
      A. why squirrels eat the sweet part of trees
      B. how to make squirrel candy from trees
      C. how squirrels get fat from candy

_____ **2.** The story mainly tells
      A. where to go hunting
      B. when the land was mostly covered by water
      C. how people can hurt things

_____ **3.** The story mainly tells
      A. how big raindrops become wet
      B. who likes to take pictures of raindrops
      C. what scientists learned about raindrops

_____ **4.** The story mainly tells
      A. which plants live outdoors
      B. how to tell when a plant is resting
      C. what rests in the summer

1. There's a lot of snow in some parts of the world. Schoolchildren in these places learn to make snowshoes. Snowshoes are big and flat. They are like duck feet. You put them on over your shoes. They are hard to walk in. But they keep your feet from sinking in the deep snow.

2. Newborn bats start life in a pocket. The mother bat makes her tail into a pocket. When a baby is born, the baby lives in it. The baby holds tight to its mother's fur. The mother hunts for food at night. The baby rides in its pocket. So baby bats get a free ride high in the sky each night.

3. What can you do if you're camping and you're caught in the rain without a tent? Rather than get wet, you can make a lean-to. First find two tree branches that are shaped like a Y. The branches should be tall and strong. Then put the two Y-shaped branches in the ground about eight feet apart. Next place a long, light stick across the two branches. Finally find many straight branches. Lean them against the cross stick on both sides. You will have a lean-to for sleeping and staying dry.

4. Have you seen any old trains? Most old trains were run by steam engine. The steam from the engine moved the train's wheels. And the steam engine gave off puffs of smoke. The puffs came out of the train's smokestack. When the train ran fast, it gave off many puffs of smoke. A train going 50 miles an hour gave off 800 smoke puffs in a minute.

_____ **1.** The story mainly tells
      A. why snow falls
      B. why some children make snowshoes
      C. who wears duck feet in cold places

_____ **2.** The story mainly tells
      A. why bats hold their mother's fur
      B. when to find bats in caves
      C. where baby bats live

_____ **3.** The story mainly tells
      A. how to make a lean-to
      B. who needs a tent
      C. what to do if it rains

_____ **4.** The story mainly tells
      A. how trains stop
      B. about trains run by steam
      C. about train wheels

1. In 2033 the all-star baseball game will be 100 years old. The first game was played in Chicago. The American League won 4–2. Vernon "Lefty" Gomez was the winning pitcher. Many years have passed since then. But Gomez will always be remembered. He was the first winning pitcher in an all-star game.

2. Charles E. Yeager was the first man to fly faster than the speed of sound. For a long time, airplanes flew slower than the speed of sound. Planes that tried to fly faster ran into sound waves. The sound waves pushed very hard against the airplanes. And they sometimes broke into pieces in the air. Then in 1947 Yeager finally flew faster than sound. His plane was strong enough to go through the sound waves.

3. In most states people who lose cats or dogs have to find the pets themselves. But not in every state. In Texas there's a man who finds missing pets. He works the same way others work to find missing people. He gets a picture of the missing pet. Then he looks everywhere for it. He questions people. He follows clues. And he slowly tracks the animal down.

4. People can now shop by telephone. When they call a certain number, a voice tells them about things to buy. It tells how much different things cost. People decide what they want. Then they place their order. Shopping by phone helps people. It saves time.

_____ **1.** The story mainly tells
      A. about a pitcher named Gomez
      B. about all-star players
      C. how to pitch

_____ **2.** The story mainly tells
      A. how old Charles Yeager was
      B. why airplanes broke apart
      C. what Charles Yeager did

_____ **3.** The story mainly tells
      A. why pets are missing
      B. who cares about missing pets
      C. how one man finds missing pets

_____ **4.** The story mainly tells
      A. who calls on the telephone
      B. how people can shop by telephone
      C. why people use the telephone to shop

1. Cattails are wild plants that grow in wet places. People use cattails in many ways. In some parts of the world, people eat the roots in salads. In other places people put the flowers in their houses. They look just like a cat's tail. People use the soft flowers to stuff chairs. They also make baskets from the long leaves.

2. Most homes in the United States have bathtubs in them. But that hasn't always been true. In fact, the first bathtub in a home was put there in 1842. Its owner was Adam Thompson. He lived in Ohio. News about his bathtub spread across the country. Doctors did not like the idea of home bathtubs. But in a few years, they changed their minds. And the bathtub soon started to be found in new homes.

3. It's hard to decide if children are more alike or more different. Each child learns at a different rate. Each child looks different from all the others. And each child acts in a different way. But children are the same in many ways. They all learn things. They all need love. They all grow. They all like to play, too.

4. People in Scotland play music on bagpipes. The bagpipe is a bag of air with five pipes. Players hold the bag under one arm. They use the arm to push the air out. Then they blow more air into the bag through one of the pipes. The player's fingers cover the holes in another pipe to make the music. Once you hear a bagpipe, you never forget its sound.

_____ **1.** The story mainly tells
     A. what people use cattails for
     B. when to eat cattail roots
     C. why cattails look pretty in a house

_____ **2.** The story mainly tells
     A. when to take a bath
     B. about an Ohio doctor
     C. about the first home bathtub

_____ **3.** The story mainly tells
     A. who looks different from everyone else
     B. why children need love and like to play
     C. how children are both different and alike

_____ **4.** The story mainly tells
     A. what a bagpipe is
     B. why a player blows on a pipe
     C. how many pipes are in the bag

1. There's an old saying: "Sleep tight and don't let the bedbugs bite." But it's no joke. Bedbugs are real. They are small insects that eat blood. They bite animals and people, too. Their bites often hurt the skin. Bedbugs can be found hiding in beds and walls. If a bedbug does bite, a person probably won't sleep tight.

2. Read the story just before this one again. Try your best to remember it. Don't peek! How many sentences can you remember? Two? Three? None? Long ago, people told many stories. These people didn't know how to read or write. So they had to remember each story. Some stories were thousands of sentences long. How did they do it? They didn't try to remember every word. They just remembered how the story went. They told the story a little differently each time, too.

3. In the fall of each year, the days grow shorter and shorter. We finally reach a time when the days and nights last about the same number of hours and minutes. During these days the full moon is called a harvest moon. It rises soon after the sun goes down. It is often a deep orange color. Since the moon is so bright, farmers have more time to harvest their crops. That's why it's called a harvest moon.

4. The Statue of Liberty is one very big woman! Her hand is 16 feet long. One of her fingers is 8 feet long. Her head is 17 feet high. And her eyes are 2 feet wide. Even her fingernails are huge. They are more than 12 inches across.

_____ **1.** The story mainly tells
   A. what bedbugs are like
   B. who gets bedbugs
   C. where bedbugs sleep

_____ **2.** The story mainly tells
   A. how many sentences you can remember
   B. who couldn't read or write
   C. how people long ago remembered stories

_____ **3.** The story mainly tells
   A. what color the harvest moon is
   B. how the harvest moon got its name
   C. when the days grow shorter

_____ **4.** The story mainly tells
   A. how long some people's fingernails are
   B. how big the Statue of Liberty is
   C. who the tallest woman in the world is

1. Mother's Day comes in May. It is the second Sunday in May. It became a holiday in 1914. Who thought of Mother's Day? It was the idea of Anna May Jarvis. She wished she had been nicer to her mother in life. So she had a service in memory of her mother. She passed out flowers to all mothers who were there. People liked the thought of a day for mothers. In a few years, Mother's Day became a holiday in the United States.

2. There are big holes in the ground in some parts of the United States. But the holes weren't always there. They were formed after people looked for water. Water is found in big underground caves. People dig wells to reach it. As they pump the ground water out, the caves dry out. Sometimes when big trucks roll over an empty cave far below, the ground falls in. This leaves a big hole.

3. Some ants live in trees. They bite through the wood and make nests and tunnels. Doors lead through the bark of the tree to the outside world. These ants keep out unwanted visitors by putting guards at the doors. Each guard has a head like a cork. They poke their heads out the door and stop up the hole.

4. Harriet Quimby was a brave woman. The new idea of flying thrilled her. So she became a pilot in 1911. The next year she became the first woman to fly across the English Channel. That great flight showed how brave she was.

_____ **1.** The story mainly tells
      A. where Anna May Jarvis lived
      B. about the month of May
      C. about the start of Mother's Day

_____ **2.** The story mainly tells
      A. what makes some holes in the ground
      B. how caves become empty
      C. how the water is pumped out

_____ **3.** The story mainly tells
      A. what kinds of trees ants live in
      B. how some ants keep out visitors
      C. how big the heads of ants are

_____ **4.** The story mainly tells
      A. how to be a pilot
      B. about flying in 1911
      C. about a brave woman pilot

1. There are many colors in the world. All colors are made from a mixture of three colors. These colors are blue, yellow, and red. They are called primary colors. Mix blue and red, and it will make purple. Blue and yellow will give you green. To make orange, mix red and yellow. Black is a mixture of blue, yellow, and red.

2. Ezra Jack Keats wrote the book *The Snowy Day*. He painted all the pictures in it. Keats taught himself to paint. Keats started painting when he was four. As a child he painted on a metal table. He would cover it with pictures. His mother showed them to her friends before cleaning up the table.

3. Long ago, people used their bodies to measure things. The first finger was used for small things. The width of that finger was a *digit*. A *span* was the width of a hand stretched out. A *cubit* was used to measure larger things. It was the length from the elbow to the tip of the longest finger.

4. A mosaic is a picture that is made from small pieces of stone or glass. The pieces are brightly colored. They are arranged to make a picture. The pieces are pressed into soft plaster. After the plaster hardens, a mosaic is made. Mosaics are used to decorate floors and walls.

_____ **1.** The story mainly tells
        A. about the way to make red
        B. how all colors are made from primary colors
        C. which colors to mix to make yellow

_____ **2.** The story mainly tells
        A. about Keats's life as a painter
        B. that Keats painted on a board
        C. that Keats didn't have paper for painting

_____ **3.** The story mainly tells
        A. how the body was used for measuring things
        B. that a *cubit* measured small things
        C. what was measured with a *digit*

_____ **4.** The story mainly tells
        A. how fast plaster hardens
        B. what kinds of pictures a mosaic can show
        C. how a mosaic is made

1. Penguins are birds. But they cannot fly. They use their wings in other ways. They use them for swimming. Their wings are like flippers. In the summer they stay cool by holding their wings away from their bodies. Their wings are put to good use even if they cannot fly.

2. The Eiffel Tower is a very big tower. It is found in Paris, France. A man named Eiffel designed it for a fair. It is made of steel. It is more than 980 feet high. It weighs more than 7,000 tons. There are 1,652 steps to the top of the tower.

3. A junk is a kind of boat. Junks sail on the seas of China and Southeast Asia. The sails of a junk have four sides. They are stretched over pieces of wood. Junks are used for fishing. Hong Kong is a very crowded city. So some people even live on their junks. A junk is sometimes a home for more than one family.

4. Emma Lazarus was a poet. She believed that America was the "land of the free." She knew that Jewish people were not treated fairly in many countries. She wanted to help them. So she wrote a poem. It is found on the Statue of Liberty. The statue and her famous poem greet the people who come to America.

_____ **1.** The story mainly tells
- **A.** where penguins live
- **B.** how penguins use their wings
- **C.** how penguins stay warm

_____ **2.** The story mainly tells
- **A.** how big the Eiffel Tower is
- **B.** how many towers there are in France
- **C.** how the Eiffel Tower is used

_____ **3.** The story mainly tells
- **A.** where most people in Hong Kong live
- **B.** about a boat called a junk
- **C.** what junks are made of

_____ **4.** The story mainly tells
- **A.** that Lazarus built the Statue of Liberty
- **B.** that Lazarus didn't want to help people
- **C.** that Lazarus wrote about freedom

1. As a boy, Pete Gray had a bad accident. He lost his right arm. Still he hoped to play big league baseball. In 1945 Pete's dream came true. He joined the St. Louis Browns. And he played in the outfield for 61 games.

2. Baboons live in groups called troops. The troops can have as many as eighty baboons in them. The strongest male is the troop leader. But some troops have more than one leader. The weaker males and all the females obey the leader. The troop moves around the plains together. Sometimes a troop will stay near a herd of antelope. The herd warns the baboons of danger. In return, the baboons scare away the leopards.

3. The lion is called the king of the jungle. But it isn't king of the jungle. In fact, the lion doesn't even live in a jungle. It lives on grassy plains.

4. Lee Treviño is a famous golfer. When he was five, his uncle gave him an old golf club. Treviño used this club to learn to play golf. He dug a hole at each end of a vacant lot. He marked both holes with sticks. He knocked golf balls back and forth. When Treviño was six, he would climb the fence of a golf course. There he would play with the same old club. Later Treviño got a job at a driving range. The owner thought Treviño was a good player. He gave Treviño his first set of golf clubs.

_____ **1.** The story mainly tells
   A. about the St. Louis Browns
   B. when an accident happened
   C. about a baseball player with one arm

_____ **2.** The story mainly tells
   A. that baboons and antelope are friends
   B. how a baboon troop lives
   C. how a baboon becomes a troop leader

_____ **3.** The story mainly tells
   A. that the lion isn't king of the jungle
   B. how lions protect their young
   C. how lions live in the jungle

_____ **4.** The story mainly tells
   A. how Treviño learned to golf
   B. that Treviño's uncle gave him a club
   C. that Treviño owned a driving range

Writing

Read each story. Think about the main idea. Write the main idea in your own words.

1. Farmers in Japan have a problem. There is not much land to farm. And there are many people to feed. Some farmers cut rows in the hillsides and grow crops there. This helps. But land for farming may always be a problem.

What is the main idea of this story?

_____

_____

2. Pocahontas was a Native American. Her father was chief of their tribe. At a young age, she learned to speak with the people who came to her land. She could explain their words to her people. She helped to keep the peace.

What is the main idea of this story?

_____

_____

3. What is a baseball worth? In 1999 a baseball was sold for more than three million dollars. It was a home-run ball. Mark McGuire set a record when he hit this ball.

What is the main idea of this story?

_____

_____

To check your answers, turn to page 60.

Prewriting

Think of a main idea that you would like to write about, such as your favorite sport, a book, or a garden. Fill in the chart below.

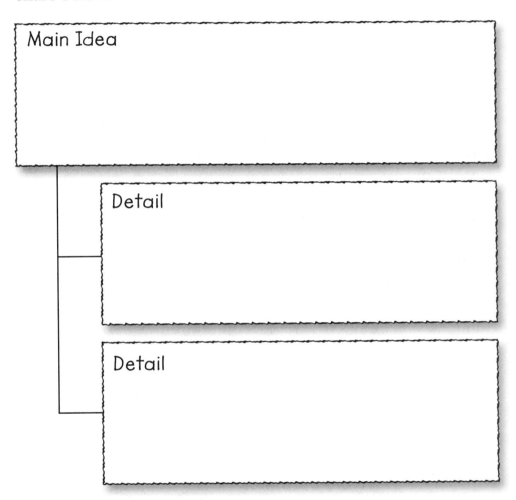

On Your Own

Now use another sheet of paper to write your story. Underline the sentence that tells the main idea.

To check your answers, turn to page 60.

1. The sparrow is the most common bird in the world. Its beak is wide and short. It has small claws on its feet. It can live almost anywhere. Sparrows are found in cities and in the country.

2. When pine cones are thrown into a campfire, they pop. The heat from the fire makes them open. When a forest is on fire, the pine cones in the trees pop. The seeds inside the cones scatter on the ground. That's why little pine trees grow quickly after a forest fire.

3. Rosa Parks always took the bus home from work. The law at that time made African Americans sit in the back of buses. So Parks sat down in the back. The driver told her and three people to give up their seats to white people. Parks refused. She was taken to jail. African Americans stopped riding buses. They thought the law was unfair. They worked to change the law. Today anyone can sit anywhere on a bus.

4. What is the biggest number that has a name? It's not a googol. A googol is the number one followed by one hundred zeroes. Maybe a googolplex is the biggest number. But a googolplex has changed. It used to be the number one followed by as many zeroes as a person could write before getting tired. Today it's the number one with a googol of zeroes. It's so big that no one has taken the time to write it!

_____ **1.** The story mainly tells
- **A.** where sparrows live
- **B.** what is strange about a sparrow
- **C.** about the most common bird

_____ **2.** The story mainly tells
- **A.** why many new trees grow after a forest fire
- **B.** that pine cones are used to build campfires
- **C.** that pine cones cause forest fires

_____ **3.** The story mainly tells
- **A.** about riding on a bus
- **B.** how Parks helped change an unfair law
- **C.** where Parks lived

_____ **4.** The story mainly tells
- **A.** who had the googol and googolplex idea
- **B.** which number may be the biggest
- **C.** that a googol is the biggest number

1. Many people think sleet and freezing rain are the same thing. But they are not. Sleet is frozen raindrops. Freezing rain is liquid raindrops. Freezing rain turns to ice when it hits the ground. Sleet does not stick to trees or wires. But freezing rain does stick to both.

2. When a star dies, a black hole may form. There is strong gravity in a black hole. Anything pulled inside the hole is twisted and stretched. Light is pulled into the hole. But light cannot get out. That is why it's called a black hole.

3. Porcupines like to eat salty things. A park ranger left his car window down. Sweat from the ranger's hands had coated the steering wheel. Sweat is salty. So what do you think happened? A porcupine ate the steering wheel!

4. Stevie Wonder has made music all of his life. When he was 2, he beat a tin pan with a spoon. So his mother bought him a play drum. Then she got him a harmonica. It had a chain. He wore it around his neck. It had 4 holes. So he could play only 4 notes. But Wonder could make music with just 4 notes. He had his first hit record at 12. He even played the harmonica on one of the songs.

_____ **1.** The story mainly tells
  A. that sleet sticks to trees and wires
  B. that sleet and freezing rain are not the same
  C. that freezing rain is more common than sleet

_____ **2.** The story mainly tells
  A. about strong gravity
  B. how a star dies
  C. what a black hole is

_____ **3.** The story mainly tells
  A. how a steering wheel got salty
  B. why the park ranger left his window open
  C. that porcupines eat almost anything salty

_____ **4.** The story mainly tells
  A. that Wonder has made music all of his life
  B. that Wonder made a record when he was 2
  C. that Wonder played the drums

1. The white settlers thought bison were a kind of ox. So they called them buffalo. Bison were hunted for their hides. The hides kept people warm. Bison meat made good food, too. The bison tongue was a special treat. But soon the big herds became small herds. Few bison were left. They were put on special land. Today bison live in protected herds.

2. Willie Mays loved baseball. But he couldn't play in the major leagues. African Americans couldn't play with white players. Mays played in the Negro Leagues. Then the New York Giants hired Mays. Mays played very well. He became a big star. He hit 660 home runs. Mays played with the Giants and the Mets. Today he is in the Baseball Hall of Fame.

3. The fruit of the squirting cucumber looks like a little pickle. Its skin stretches as it grows. Pressure builds inside the fruit. When the fruit is ripe, it falls off the stem. This opens a hole at one end. The seeds squirt out from the hole. They can fly as far as 25 feet!

4. Fred Morrison invented the Frisbee. He wanted to make a pie tin into a toy. His first metal toy was too heavy. It didn't fly well. So he tried plastic. It sailed through the air. He sold the toy to a company that named it Pluto Platter. Later people played a game called Frisbie-ing. They threw pie tins from the Frisbie Pie Company. The toy company liked the game. So it changed the spelling and called the toy a Frisbee.

Steck-Vaughn • Comprehension Skills Series

_____ **1.** The story mainly tells
  A. about bison
  B. how bad bison tongue tasted
  C. that bison hides were not any good

_____ **2.** The story mainly tells
  A. how long Mays played baseball
  B. that Mays played for the Mets
  C. that Mays was a great baseball player

_____ **3.** The story mainly tells
  A. about a fruit that squirts its seeds
  B. about a kind of pickle
  C. where cucumber seeds come from

_____ **4.** The story mainly tells
  A. how to spell Frisbee
  B. that Frisbee was fun to play
  C. how the Frisbee was invented

Main Idea • Level B

U N I T

16

1. Doug Simpson and his dog Nick went camping in Arizona. One day Nick ran away. For two weeks Doug looked for Nick. But it was no use. So Doug went home to Washington. Four months later a dog limped his way to Doug. Doug couldn't believe that this skinny dog was Nick. Then the dog licked Doug's hand. Doug knew it was Nick. Nick's trip home was more than one thousand miles!

2. Long ago in China, some lotus plants grew in a lake. But then the lake dried up. Some seeds stayed in the mud. Hundreds of years later, a scientist dug up the seeds. He saved them in a box for thirty years. An American took two of the seeds home. He planted the seeds. Soon lotus plants grew from seeds more than a thousand years old!

3. Italians invented eyeglasses in the 1200s. Through the years many things have held them in place. At first people held the eyeglasses to their eyes with their hands. In the 1720s frames that rested on the nose and ears were made. But the ear pieces were straight. Later, people bent them for a better fit.

4. Zora Neale Hurston grew up in a small town. The town people liked sitting on the porch of the general store. There they told stories. Hurston loved listening to their stories. She loved the folktales. When Hurston grew up, she became a writer. She wrote stories about the folktales she had heard as a child.

Steck-Vaughn • Comprehension Skills Series

_____ **1.** The story mainly tells
     A. how Doug got home from Arizona
     B. how a dog made a long trip home
     C. that Doug never found his dog

_____ **2.** The story mainly tells
     A. how plants grew from very old seeds
     B. how to grow lotus plants
     C. that it's best to keep lotus seeds in a box

_____ **3.** The story mainly tells
     A. how eyeglasses changed through the years
     B. that eyeglasses were invented in 1720
     C. how to buy eyeglasses that fit well

_____ **4.** The story mainly tells
     A. how Hurston sat on a porch
     B. how Hurston told folktales as a child
     C. how Hurston used folktales to write

1. The bristlecone pine tree is one of the oldest plants on Earth. Most pine trees live for about 250 years. The bristlecone pine can live more than 4,000 years. It is also one of the slowest growing plants. One tree took 1,500 years to grow 15 feet.

2. Early settlers made drinks from herbs and weeds. They added yeast to the drinks. The yeast made the drinks fizz. Native Americans also made drinks. But they made drinks from roots and barks. Together the settlers and the Native Americans made a new drink. They mixed roots and barks with yeast. They invented the first root beer!

3. The first bus service began in 1662. Blaise Pascal owned the first buses. The buses ran in Paris, France. But his buses were not like buses today. Pascal's buses were pulled by horses. Each bus carried eight riders.

4. A moon is not the same as a planet. A planet is a world that moves around the Sun. A moon is much smaller than a planet. It moves around a planet. All but two of our planets have moons. These are Venus and Mercury. Earth and Pluto each have one moon. Jupiter has 16 moons!

_____ **1.** The story mainly tells
   A. where bristlecone pine trees grow
   B. about a kind of old tree that grows slowly
   C. how pine trees don't live long

_____ **2.** The story mainly tells
   A. how root beer was invented
   B. about drinks that the settlers made
   C. that yeast makes drinks fizz

_____ **3.** The story mainly tells
   A. that Pascal had only eight buses
   B. about the first bus service
   C. how bus service was slow in 1662

_____ **4.** The story mainly tells
   A. that Earth has two moons
   B. that most planets don't have moons
   C. how a moon and a planet are different

1. The first person went up into space in 1961. His name was Yuri Gagarin. He was Russian. His spacecraft was the *Vostok 1*. It circled Earth just one time. Gagarin was in space for less than two hours.

2. How are a toad and a frog different? A toad spends more time out of water than a frog. Its skin is duller, rougher, and drier. The legs of a toad are shorter, too. A toad cannot jump as far as a frog. A frog lays its eggs in a jelly-like mass. A toad lays its eggs in strings. It wraps the eggs around the stems of water plants.

3. Sitting Bull was a Sioux leader. He didn't want his people to lose their land. He told the tribes to join against the white settlers. That way they might keep their homeland. In 1876 some tribes camped near the Little Bighorn River. General Custer and his troops charged the group. Sitting Bull's men destroyed the troops. It was a great win for Native Americans.

4. The kiwi is a strange bird. It lives in New Zealand. The kiwi has tiny wings. But it cannot fly. It is covered with feathers that look like hair. Its bill is six inches long. Its nostrils are found at the end of its bill. It uses its bill to smell worms in the soil. The kiwi comes out only at night. It lives in holes near the roots of trees.

_____ **1.** The story mainly tells
  A. about the first manned spaceflight
  B. that *Vostok 1* was a planet
  C. which American was first in space

_____ **2.** The story mainly tells
  A. where a frog lays its eggs
  B. how a frog and a toad are different
  C. how far a toad can jump

_____ **3.** The story mainly tells
  A. how Custer won the Battle of Little Bighorn
  B. that Sitting Bull was a peaceful man
  C. how Sitting Bull's words helped the Sioux

_____ **4.** The story mainly tells
  A. about the kiwi bird
  B. that a kiwi does not have feathers
  C. how far a kiwi can fly

1. A geyser is a spring that throws out jets of hot water and steam. One geyser is found in Yellowstone National Park. It is called Old Faithful. It got its name because it spouts once an hour. Since it was found, it has never missed an hour. It was found in 1870!

2. One animal has a nose six feet long. That's as big as a tall person! This long-nosed animal is an elephant. An elephant's nose is called a trunk. It lets an elephant breathe and smell. An elephant sucks water with its trunk. Then it gives itself a shower. It also uses its trunk to put food in its mouth.

3. In movie history, Ramon Novarro is known as a great star from Mexico. Like many movie stars, he changed his name. His real name was Ramon Gil Samoniegos.

4. Curling began in Scotland. It was played 500 years ago. It is a fun sport. It is played by sweeping ice. Each player has a large stone and a broom. The stones have handles on them. They weigh 35 pounds each. The players slide the stones across the ice toward a target. They sweep the ice in front of the stones to make them travel farther.

_____ **1.** The story mainly tells
- **A.** about the age of Old Faithful
- **B.** what Yellowstone National Park looks like
- **C.** about a geyser called Old Faithful

_____ **2.** The story mainly tells
- **A.** about an animal with a very long nose
- **B.** why an elephant's nose is called a trunk
- **C.** how an elephant can give itself a shower

_____ **3.** The story mainly tells
- **A.** about movies to see
- **B.** about a great movie star from Mexico
- **C.** how to change your name

_____ **4.** The story mainly tells
- **A.** what a curling stone is made of
- **B.** how the sport of curling is played
- **C.** that curling is played in Texas

1. Did you know that the world's largest bird can't fly? Can you name the bird? It's an ostrich. Why can't it fly? It's too big. An ostrich can be more than eight feet tall. It can weigh more than 330 pounds. It lives in the grasslands of Africa.

2. How fast does the human heart beat? In most people, the heart beats seventy times a minute. A heart rate of fifty beats a minute is normal. But so is a heart rate of one hundred. A healthy heart beats between fifty and one hundred times a minute. A heart beats about three thousand million times in a lifetime!

3. There are eight notes on a musical scale. Each scale starts and ends with the same letter. One scale is *C, D, E, F, G, A, B, C.* From one *C* to the next *C* is called an octave. *Octave* comes from the Greek word *okto* meaning "eight."

4. Many babies were born at home in 1893. Esther Cleveland was born at home in that year. Her home was famous. It was the White House. Her father was President Grover Cleveland. Until that time, no other child of a president had been born in the White House.

_____ **1.** The story mainly tells
   A. which zoos have ostriches
   B. about the largest bird in the world
   C. how well ostriches hunt

_____ **2.** The story mainly tells
   A. about normal heart rates for humans
   B. how to measure your heartbeat
   C. about the heart rate during a heart attack

_____ **3.** The story mainly tells
   A. what a _C_ note is
   B. how many scales there are
   C. what an octave is

_____ **4.** The story mainly tells
   A. how Cleveland was elected
   B. when Esther Cleveland was born
   C. about a baby born in the White House

1. Jacques Cartier was a French explorer. He made three trips to Canada. Cartier tried to find out what the natives called their land. He asked a few of them. But they didn't understand him. They thought he was asking about their village. So they said, "Kanada." That was their word for *village*. So the huge country of Canada was named after a little village!

2. There are many stories about King Arthur. He always met with his knights at a table. It was huge. It seated 150 people. At that time the most important person sat at the head of a table. But King Arthur's table was round. So there wasn't any head of the table. All the seats were equal!

3. Most fish lay eggs. Some fish leave their eggs to hatch by themselves. Other fish watch over their eggs. Mouthbrooders keep their eggs safe. They keep their eggs in their mouths. They even keep their young there. They can eat without swallowing any eggs or young!

4. George Herman Ruth liked to play baseball. His nickname was Babe. In 1914 he played for the Boston Red Sox. Ruth was just 19 years old. He played ball for 21 years. Why was he the king of home runs? Because he hit 714 home runs. His record was not broken for 40 years.

_____ **1.** The story mainly tells
     A. which countries Cartier explored
     B. how Canada was named after a village
     C. that the natives didn't like Cartier

_____ **2.** The story mainly tells
     A. how many knights King Arthur had
     B. why King Arthur had a round table
     C. that there are 150 stories about King Arthur

_____ **3.** The story mainly tells
     A. where most fish lay their eggs
     B. how many eggs a mouthbrooder lays
     C. about the safe place of a mouthbrooder

_____ **4.** The story mainly tells
     A. what a great baseball player Ruth was
     B. that George Ruth changed his name
     C. that Ruth retired in 1935

1. Peeling an onion can make your eyes water. People try many things to keep from crying. Some people hold an onion under running water. Others try wearing goggles. But goggles make the cook look silly!

2. The thigh bone is the biggest bone in the body. It connects the hip bone to the knee bone. Why does it need to be big and strong? It has to support the weight of the body. It must hold up the leg muscles, too. It needs to be long so that the legs can take wide steps.

3. Many years ago, a company made a new tape. It was called Scotch tape. It was meant for use with clear wrapping. But some found other uses for the tape. They used it to mend old toys and torn clothing. They used it for many things. Later many companies made the same type of clear tape. They gave it new names. And people bought these new tapes. But the first name given to the clear tape stuck. So now when people use clear tape, they call it Scotch tape.

4. Do you like yo-yos? Where do you think they started? Some people think that the yo-yo began in the United States. But the first yo-yo came to the United States in 1929. It came from the Philippines. The word *yo-yo* means "come come" in the Filipino language.

_____ **1.** The story mainly tells
      A. why onions make people cry
      B. ways to peel an onion without crying
      C. ways to use goggles

_____ **2.** The story mainly tells
      A. that the biggest bone is found in the arm
      B. why the thigh bone is so big
      C. how bones help a person walk

_____ **3.** The story mainly tells
      A. how clear tape works
      B. why old toys are taped
      C. why clear tapes are called Scotch tape

_____ **4.** The story mainly tells
      A. where the yo-yo started
      B. that the yo-yo was invented in 1939
      C. how to say *come* in the Filipino language

1. What is the difference between a donkey and a mule? A donkey looks much like a horse. But it has long ears. It has a big head and a short mane. A donkey has two stripes on its back and shoulders. A mule has a horse for a mother and a donkey for a father. A mule is bigger than a donkey. It is stronger, too. And a mule is not as nervous as a donkey.

2. Some humans can run at a speed of close to 30 miles an hour. Pet cats can reach the same speed. But cats can go at that speed much longer than humans. So when people want their cats, they shouldn't chase after them. The cats will often prove to be too fast to catch.

3. Big storms can lift all sorts of things in the air. Things can be carried for hundreds of miles. In 1900 there was a huge storm in England. After the storm it rained frogs and bugs! But it has never rained cats and dogs!

4. When a baby pelican is hungry, it looks for one of its parents. It taps on the parent's bill. The parent opens its mouth. The baby sticks its head inside. Fish that the parent has eaten come up. The baby feeds on this fish. The baby stays in the nest for ten weeks. It will weigh more than its parents. The young bird will live on the extra fat while it learns to catch fish.

_____ **1.** The story mainly tells
     A. how a donkey and a mule are different
     B. that a donkey has shorter ears than a mule
     C. that donkeys are bigger than mules

_____ **2.** The story mainly tells
     A. how fast humans and cats run
     B. when humans chase cats
     C. what makes cats run so fast

_____ **3.** The story mainly tells
     A. about the time it rained cats and dogs
     B. that a storm made it rain frogs and insects
     C. about the number of frogs in England in 1900

_____ **4.** The story mainly tells
     A. how pelicans catch fish
     B. about baby pelicans
     C. where pelicans build their nests

1. Babies use both hands. But many babies use one hand more than the other. This hand may become the preferred one. How can you tell? Lay a baby on its back. Notice which side the baby faces. If the baby looks to the right most of the time, it will probably be right-handed. What does it mean if the baby faces left more often? The baby will most likely be left-handed.

2. Do you ever wonder how we taste things? We owe our sense of taste to our taste buds. We have nine thousand taste buds just on our tongue alone. There are also taste buds on the roof of our mouth. We even have taste buds on the back of our throat.

3. Sand isn't as quiet as it may seem to be. It can make sounds. Sand whistles, squeaks, and booms. It whistles when someone walks on it. Try running on sand. You'll hear it squeak. It whistles and squeaks when a stick is jammed into it. Next time you are at the beach, build a sand castle. You'll hear it boom when it falls.

4. Were you born after 1985? If so, how long do you expect to live? Most people born after 1985 can expect to live more than 70 years. Of course, this is just a guess based on past records. By the way, females can expect to live about 6 years longer than males. That's taken from past records, too!

_____ **1.** The story mainly tells
       A. how to tell right- from left-handed babies
       B. that babies use their hands for many things
       C. that there are more left-handed babies

_____ **2.** The story mainly tells
       A. why we can taste only sweet things
       B. that we taste through our nose
       C. where taste buds are found

_____ **3.** The story mainly tells
       A. that sand is very quiet
       B. where sand comes from
       C. about the noises that sand makes

_____ **4.** The story mainly tells
       A. why people live to be 70
       B. how long you might expect to live
       C. about the health of females

1. Sometimes people can't remember their dreams. But everyone dreams while sleeping. Most people dream two hours every night. In that time they have four or five dreams. Each dream is longer than the dream before. You can tell when someone is dreaming. Their eyeballs move back and forth under their closed eyelids.

2. A snake doesn't open its mouth to stick out its tongue. The snake's jaw has a notch that lets the tongue move in and out. The tongue is not poisonous. It is used by the snake to smell. The tongue picks up air and carries it back into the mouth. There are two small holes on the roof of the mouth. It is these holes that smell the air.

3. Do you like bananas? Have you ever seen them growing outside? Bananas grow in bunches. A bunch of bananas is called a hand. Bananas grow in big hands. Each banana is called a finger. Each finger grows upward.

4. In 1904, New York opened its subway for train travel in the city. The fast trains took 28 minutes. They went from one end of the city to the other. Some trains made more stops. They took 46 minutes. It cost five cents to ride the train. People loved the ride and the price.

_____ **1.** The story mainly tells
      A. how much sleep people need
      B. how often people dream
      C. what dreams mean

_____ **2.** The story mainly tells
      A. how a snake uses its tongue to smell
      B. that a snake's tongue is poisonous
      C. that a snake has three holes on its tongue

_____ **3.** The story mainly tells
      A. how bananas grow
      B. how to eat bananas with your fingers
      C. how the banana got its name

_____ **4.** The story mainly tells
      A. how to travel in New York
      B. about the 1904 New York subway
      C. when the subway made stops

Writing

Read each story. Think about the main idea. Write the main idea in your own words.

1. In 1987 an 18-month-old girl fell into a well in her yard. Her name was Jessica McClure. She was trapped there. People worked to save her. It took more than two days. But she was pulled free. Jessica was lucky to be alive!

What is the main idea of this story?

_____

_____

2. We think of the White House as the home of the President. But this was not always true. George Washington did not live in the White House. He lived in New York.

What is the main idea of this story?

_____

_____

3. Gail Devers won a gold medal in the 1992 Olympic Games. She was one of the fastest women in the world. She had come a long way. Her high school had no track team or coach. So Gail had to train herself.

What is the main idea of this story?

_____

_____

To check your answers, turn to page 60.

Prewriting

Think of a main idea that you would like to write about, such as a family member, a hero, or a place to go. Fill in the chart below.

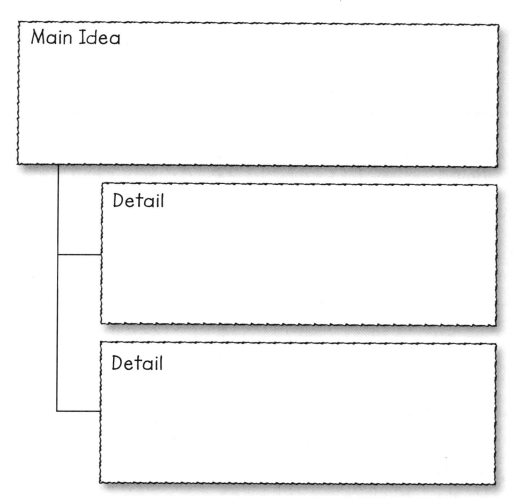

Main Idea

Detail

Detail

On Your Own

Now use another sheet of paper to write your story. Underline the sentence that tells the main idea.

To check your answers, turn to page 60.

Check Yourself

How to Choose a Main Idea, Page 3

Detail 1: bathtub, car

Detail 2: store

Detail 3: music while you sing a song

Detail 4: recording

Detail 5: take it home and surprise

Main Idea: Here's how you can become a singing star!

Practice Finding the Main Idea, Page 4

2. The correct answer is c. All the sentences are about the Bill of Rights. The first two sentences tell what the Bill of Rights is about. The last two sentences add details about why it is important.

To check your answers to pages 6–29, see page 61.

Writing, Page 30

Possible answers include:

1. Farmers in Japan don't have much land.
2. Pocahontas helped her people.
3. A famous baseball can be worth a lot of money.

Writing, Page 31

Check that you underlined your main idea.
Check that you used two details.

To check your answers to pages 32–57, see page 62.

Writing, Page 58

Possible answers include:

1. Jessica McClure was lucky to be alive.
2. Not all Presidents lived in the White House.
3. Gail Devers trained herself to be a runner.

Writing, Page 59

Check that you underlined your main idea.
Check that you used two details.

Steck-Vaughn • Comprehension Skills Series

Check Yourself

Unit 1 pp. 6–7	Unit 2 pp. 8–9	Unit 3 pp. 10–11	Unit 4 pp. 12–13	Unit 5 pp. 14–15	Unit 6 pp. 16–17	Unit 7 pp. 18–19	Unit 8 pp. 20–21	Unit 9 pp. 22–23	Unit 10 pp. 24–25	Unit 11 pp. 26–27	Unit 12 pp. 28–29
1. A	**1.** A	**1.** A	**1.** A	**1.** B	**1.** A	**1.** A	**1.** A	**1.** C	**1.** B	**1.** B	**1.** C
2. A	**2.** C	**2.** B	**2.** C	**2.** C	**2.** C	**2.** C	**2.** C	**2.** A	**2.** A	**2.** A	**2.** B
3. C	**3.** B	**3.** A	**3.** C	**3.** A	**3.** C	**3.** C	**3.** B	**3.** B	**3.** A	**3.** B	**3.** A
4. B	**4.** B	**4.** B	**4.** B	**4.** B	**4.** B	**4.** A	**4.** B	**4.** C	**4.** C	**4.** C	**4.** A

Main Idea • Level B

Unit 13 pp. 32–33	Unit 14 pp. 34–35	Unit 15 pp. 36–37	Unit 16 pp. 38–39	Unit 17 pp. 40–41	Unit 18 pp. 42–43	Unit 19 pp. 44–45	Unit 20 pp. 46–47	Unit 21 pp. 48–49	Unit 22 pp. 50–51	Unit 23 pp. 52–53	Unit 24 pp. 54–55	Unit 25 pp. 56–57
1. C	1. B	1. A	1. B	1. B	1. A	1. C	1. B	1. B	1. B	1. A	1. A	1. B
2. A	2. C	2. C	2. A	2. A	2. B	2. A	2. A	2. B	2. B	2. A	2. C	2. A
3. B	3. C	3. A	3. A	3. B	3. C	3. B	3. C	3. C	3. C	3. B	3. C	3. A
4. B	4. A	4. C	4. C	4. C	4. A	4. B	4. C	4. A	4. A	4. B	4. B	4. B